Why Pilgrimage?

by
David Baldwin

GW00703505

All booklets are published thanks to the
generous support of the members of the
Catholic Truth Society

CATHOLIC TRUTH SOCIETY
PUBLISHERS TO THE HOLY SEE

This book is for you, Fellow Pilgrim,
as we ever contemplate

This hill, though high, I covet to ascend;
The difficulty will not me offend.
For I perceive the way to life lies here.
Come, pluck up, heart; let's neither faint nor fear.
Better, though difficult, the right way to go,
Than wrong, though easy, where the end is woe.

(John Bunyan, *The Pilgrim's Progress*)

4

Contents

All rights reserved. First published 2015 by The Incorporated Catholic Truth Society, 40-46 Harleyford Road London SE11 5AY Tel: 020 7640 0042 Fax: 020 7640 0046. Copyright © 2015 The Incorporated Catholic Truth Society.

ISBN 978 1 78469 077 9

Inside images: Shutterstock except *Statue of Our Lady of Walsingham* courtesy of Catholic Church of England and Wales/Marcin Mazur, Flickr.

Introduction

Recent years have seen rising numbers of pilgrims of all faiths seeking out their holy places. Set in the context of today's overburdened and fractured world, there seems to be a deep yearning and a restless desire to seek consolation, solace, healing, affirmation, peace, forgiveness, reassurance - whether through that encounter on the pilgrim journey, or at the destination, or both - that would bring about a sense of fulfillment and a deeper understanding of self.

This applies equally to the Christian pilgrim, as evidenced by the millions who go every year to those well known, cherished pilgrim destinations such as the Holy Land, Rome, Lourdes, Fatima, Guadalupe, Santiago de Compostela. But there are many others less well known or locally popular places of pilgrimage - which, of course, are just as valid or appealing.

This small book is about pilgrimage. It aims to give insights, ideas and inspiration, with a view to setting you - or continuing you - on your pilgrim journeys!

Specifically, we will look at reasons for going on pilgrimage, at preparing to set out, at expectations and experiences en route, on arrival, and having returned home. We will briefly look at the history of pilgrimage, and its enduring appeal over the ages. We will then consider potential destinations, grouped into: the Three Principal Destinations, Marian Shrines, Places of the Great Saints, and finally a miscellany, covering other places. "Reasons to go" have been proposed, but are by no means definitive or exclusive - your reason for going on your pilgrimage will be very personal to you.

We hope all this will give you a practical perception and assist your approach and planning. It may also whet the appetite of those who are generally looking, or those who may not know much about, or yet to engage, in pilgrimage.

To further your interest or researches we have listed at the back of the book some key contact references, as well as relevant CTS publications.

Buen Camino! - be richly blessed on your pilgrim journeys!

> *Put no faith in your own perception;*
> *in every course you take, have him in mind:*
> *he will see that your paths are smooth.*
>
> *(Pr 3:5,6)*

Why Pilgrimage?

Pilgrimages have as their goal the tent of the personal meeting with God and with oneself. Lost in the multiplicity of daily anxieties and realities, people need to discover themselves through reflection, meditation, prayer, an examination of conscience, silence.

(Pontifical Council for Migrants, *The Pilgrimage in the Great Jubilee*)

A sure sign of our frenetically paced times is that occasional pervasive yearning to somehow "get away from it all", and leave our worries, preoccupations and burdens behind. Whilst our much anticipated annual holiday may seem the obvious remedy, there is another possibility worth considering - not necessarily as an alternative, but certainly one which may offer other avenues, other experiences, and provide fulfilment of a differing and more enduring kind - and that is pilgrimage.

In many ways this could be the complete antithesis of your holiday ideal, where, on pilgrimage, you go not as the paying customer on a constant "value for money" quest, but rather as supplicant, with muted expectations on the material front. One where the setbacks and frustrations normally encountered on holiday can be embraced as positive and strengthening experiences. But one where there could also be a big plus side, with joyful, unexpected, exquisite or humbling moments coming your way.

What is pilgrimage?

At its simplest, pilgrimage is a physical journey, *your* journey. But it is a journey undertaken with *spiritual intent*, usually heading for a destination of religious significance. In the words of the Marqués de Tamaron, then Spanish ambassador to the United Kingdom, in his preface to the CTS booklet on Santiago, "Pilgrimage implies a voyage of self-discovery and a search for something greater and beyond oneself". But please do not let the prospect of "spirituality" put you off, because there are *no rules, no mystery, no limitations* to making pilgrimage. Although being an integral part of your physical journey, the spiritual content can be as light or as intense, as passive or as active as you desire; just open yourself to the Holy Spirit in hope and humility. It is all about attitude and approach, acceptance and authenticity, rather than high expectation.

> *Blessed are those who find their strength in you,*
> *whose hearts are set on pilgrimage.*
>
> (*Ps* 84.5)

As I said, there are no rules: your pilgrimage can be as long or as short as you wish, local or long distance. You can make or repeat as many as you like, at short or no notice, or with as much preparation as required. It is not necessarily meant to be a "sackcloth and ashes" experience (unless you are specifically going on a penitential journey!): you are allowed to enjoy yourself! You will likely meet interesting folk, and encounter unusual and unexpected situations en route. It also doesn't matter by what means you make that journey - foot, bike, bus, train, car, plane, horse, wheelchair, or any combination of these. Or, in complete contrast, you can journey interiorly in thought and prayer; and that you can truly do at no notice and at any time.

Why go on pilgrimage?

There could be many reasons for going on a pilgrimage. For some, there will be an obvious, single, clear purpose; for others, the purpose may be more complex. There will be the initial reason or reasons that you may discern as the explicit purpose of your journey; other reasons may surface (sometimes quite unexpectedly) during your journey, and others may not reveal themselves until long afterwards.

Part of it may be a desire to disconnect or distance oneself from over-familiar or maybe upsetting or distracting surroundings, to find "neutral ground", to try and "get away from it all". Part (or maybe all) may be about trying to cope with bereavement, going through a difficult patch in life, wishing to discern next steps, or simply seeking a completely different experience for a while - taking time out of time. Others may go for the spiritual uplift of the journey itself, or to venerate a favourite saint, or experience some sublime place or shrine, or to make a specific request or intercession; or to seek physical or spiritual healing, reconciliation or forgiveness.

But, with that desire to get away from it all, it may be important not to regard pilgrimage as the total escape or the only means of averting or solving issues – more an opportunity to confront them, face up to yourself and to whatever may be besetting you. Or, maybe going on a voyage of deeper self-discovery – of yourself, your faith, relationships. But above all, placing yourself totally in the hands of a compassionate, listening and caring God.

> *The Lord says this, "Put yourselves on the ways of long ago, enquire about the ancient paths: which was the good way? Take it then, and you will find rest."*
>
>   *(Jr 6:16)*

Pilgrim experiences

Whilst you think about or prepare yourselves for your pilgrimage, or on the journey itself and afterwards, it may be helpful if I share some experiences of my first serious pilgrimage: walking the thousand-year-old pilgrim route through France and Spain, along the Way of St James to Santiago de Compostela. As it was over some distance (nine hundred miles) and time (nine weeks) I learnt a lot, and my experience may be relevant to your own journey, however you go, however long you take, and to whatever destination. I do not mean to pre-empt any of the unexpected surprises, discoveries or pleasures that you could encounter - they will manifest themselves in their own unique, and sometimes surprising way - but more to give an inkling as to the possibilities.

With these experiences I will link the spiritual goals of pilgrimage as expressed in the rich language of the Church's document *Pilgrimage in the Great Jubilee*. In this text, the use of the biblical word "tent" is set in the Old Testament context of the "meeting place with God" (cf *Ex* 33:7).

I had heard only in rather vague terms about Santiago and the Way of St James, and it was only a chance encounter with the Travel Section of a newspaper that suddenly pulled it all into focus, fuelling my desire to walk this pilgrim route. I was beginning to return fully to my faith, and saw this as an ideal and providential opportunity of affirmation by going on a full-blown, "old-fashioned" walking pilgrimage. The lesson here is that the prompting for your pilgrimage may come at an unexpected moment and from completely unexpected (and secular) sources!

Reasons

My main spiritual reasons for going were to make an overt profession of my faith, with elements of thanksgiving and atonement, and to reinforce my fresh commitment to the Christian life. I also saw it as a chance thoroughly to plumb the depths of my spirit.

There were other more material reasons: travel to foreign places, new experiences, meeting people and hearing their stories, stunning scenery, and (I hoped) some sunny days and good food. I was looking forward to life in the slow, but not necessarily comfortable, lane.

On the other side of the coin, I knew I was taking a risk; for here I was, middle-aged, middle-of-the-road, middle-England, about to launch off on foot, on my own, on a nine hundred mile journey across France and Spain, with little knowledge of the language, knowing that accommodation and conditions would be very basic, with invariably crowded, mixed dormitories, packed with foreigners, and knowing also that at some stage it would rain (in fact it also snowed!). There is a lesson here: yes, take a risk, but put it in God's hands!

> The aim, towards which the pilgrim's itinerary is directed, is first of all the tent of meeting with God. Isaiah already mentioned these words of God: "My house will be called a house of prayer for all peoples".
> (*Is* 56:7) (*Pilgrimage in the Great Jubilee*)

Alone or in company?

On this occasion, I chose to go alone. This is one of the major practical considerations when planning your pilgrimage: to go alone, or in company. In company could mean going with one friend or several, or with family, or with a more corporate group such as your parish or diocese, or joining the homogeneity of a pilgrim group with a tour company. All have pluses and minuses.

Going alone allows you to go at your own speed, to follow your own agenda, and not be limited by any constraints (imagined or real!) of your companions; but you obviously bear the full weight and responsibility for every aspect of your journey. When travelling solo, I learned very early on that actually I need never be alone. One always felt quite free to join an individual or a group, walk and talk with them, and equally free to peel off, without offence being taken on either side.

Going with friends or family has the obvious advantage of sharing organisation, as well as giving mutual support and enjoying shared experiences. Going with a parish or diocese will strengthen and affirm your community spirit, and again eases organisation. Going with a tour company eliminates the burden of organisation and responsibility altogether, and allows you to benefit from expert knowledge and guidance, as well as to gain new friends. But group outings, of whatever size, do demand a certain compliance with a programme and entail consideration for others, things which should be regarded as part of the pilgrim experience!

On my various pilgrim journeys, I have done all of these, with variations such as, for instance, privately extending a stay after touring with a group to explore places in more detail.

En route

Early on I rather resented, when walking and wishing to be alone, if someone came up alongside for company. But that little voice inside started saying, "The very least you can do is give a civil greeting and make them feel welcome". And of course that was the message: that this encounter was not by chance, so I should engage more deeply, which I started to do. I had some lovely exchanges, and met some memorable people. And yes, I did talk with those dealing with bereavement, mending fractured relationships, deciding important next moves, or simply just enjoying the experience.

> Pilgrimages also lead to the tent of meeting with humankind. All religions of the world have their own holy itineraries and their holy cities. In every place of the earth, God himself becomes a meeting with the pilgrim and proclaims a universal convocation to participate fully in the joy of Abraham.
>
> (*Pilgrimage in the Great Jubilee*)

I also soon learned how judgmental I was. Early on, there were two men walking together, one older, with a younger man who was partially bald but had a pony-tail. Middle England at that stage did not like partially bald men with pony tails! I decided to stay clear of these two. But inevitably our paths literally crossed, and conversation had to be started. They were French, and it transpired that they were father and son on a heartfelt journey of reconciliation after many years of bitter estrangement. How internally shamed I felt! They proved delightful company, and along the route we became good friends. That one encounter tempered my attitude completely regarding my fellow human beings.

> The shrine is also the tent of meeting in reconciliation. There, in fact, the pilgrim's conscience is moved; there he confesses his sins; there he is forgiven and forgives; there he becomes a new creature through the sacrament of reconciliation; there he experiences divine mercy and grace.
>
> (*Pilgrimage in the Great Jubilee*)

By engaging with the hugger-mugger of pilgrim life, I soon realised a humbling process was gently underway here, as one had to adapt to communal life and basic circumstances. It also became obvious early on that consideration for others was a major factor. I experienced nothing but courtesy and selflessness, witnessing many acts of kindness along the way. I pray I gave back as good as I got. And these were people from many nations and ages; singles, couples, groups, all bound by a sense of sharing this unique and singular experience.

> Pilgrimages may also be the tent of meeting with charity. A charity that is first of all that of God who loved us first by sending his Son into the world. This love is not manifested only in Christ's gift as a victim of expiation for our sins (cf 1 *Jn* 4:10), but also in the miraculous signs that heal and console, as Christ himself did during his earthly pilgrimage, and which are still repeated in the history of shrines.
>
> (*Pilgrimage in the Great Jubilee*)

How wonderful it is, how pleasant, for God's people to live together in harmony.

(*Ps* 133:1)

Spiritual Encounters

One of my most earnest desires on this pilgrim journey was to encounter, in some way, the presence of God:

My soul is thirsting for God, the God of my life: when can I enter and see the face of God?

(*Ps* 41:3).

I was not in any way asking for something as dramatic as St Paul's experience, but maybe at least a humble revelation or some small manifestation? On about week six, as I was walking, I was beginning to fear that this was not going to happen. Then I was suddenly prompted to recall very clearly the previous evening in our *refugio*. Just after our communal evening meal, a Spanish man came into the common room with a small bag, which he opened, and taking out minor medical equipment, asked, "Would anyone like me to tend to your feet?"

After the initial surprise, he was soon fully in business, fixing the many unpleasant foot-borne afflictions of the pilgrim. He had a full-time day job, and this was something he did most evenings. At one stage he had walked the Camino, and wanted to give something back. Full realisation then hit me, with simple but wondrous revelation: "Yes, I *have* seen the face of God - it was there, in that man and his humble ministry!"

I then cast my mind back along my journey, to all the small acts of kindness and consideration I had already encountered, remembering particularly the two families in Estaing who had given up their lucrative professional lives to run a pilgrim hostel.

But God was also plainly around me all the time - in his glorious Creation: the liquid song of nightingales, the vast, hushed, cathedral-like forests, the non-stop display of exquisite wild flowers in their miniature perfection. One time, when I knew I was nearing the Pyrenees, I topped a brow, and there laid before me on that perfect sunlit day was my first sight of those majestic, snow peaked mountains. I was totally overwhelmed by God's glory at that sight, and just gave thanks in spontaneous prayer.

> While persons are on pilgrimage they also have the chance to enter the tent of cosmic meeting with God. Shrines [*and the routes to them*] are often located in places with an extraordinary panorama; they manifest greatly fascinating artistic forms; they concentrate in themselves ancient historical memories; they are expressions of popular and refined culture. It is therefore necessary for pilgrimages not to exclude this dimension of the spirit.
>
> (*Pilgrimage in the Great Jubilee*)

Another sublime moment was coming across some young French mountain bikers, with whom I had previously exchanged cheery greetings, gathered on a hill-top, obviously in prayer overlooking what might have been a scene from Eden.

> *I looked down over the immense plain*
> *Where I sought the Master and King,*
> *And I cried, seeing the pure wave,*
> *The starry azure, the flower, and the bird:*
> *"Bright nature, if I do not see God,*
> *You are nothing to me but a vast tomb"*
>
> (St Thérèse of Lisieux)

Chapels, churches, shrines and wayside crucifixes and grottos were generally plentiful along the Way. Peace, utter peace and tranquillity, a complete feeling of calm and serenity reigned in these still, holy places, where I stopped just to meditate, wonder, pray. I also took every opportunity to attend Mass, sometimes at the end of a day's walk, when it was specifically celebrated for pilgrims en route.

> The goal of pilgrimages must be the tent of the Eucharistic meeting with Christ. If the Bible is the book of pilgrims *par excellence,* the Eucharist is the bread that sustains them on their way, as it was for Elijah on his ascent to Horeb
> (cf. 1 *K* 19:4-8) (*Pilgrimage in the Great Jubilee*)

Know yourself

I think everybody has their own way of looking at their lives as some kind of pilgrimage... Everybody's got their own definition. Mine, I suppose, is to know myself.

(Eric Clapton)

We now come to what was the most challenging part, and partially why I was there: having a good, honest look at myself. I will not say I found it easy, but early on I was prompted with the notion that with our many masks, we can fool anyone at any or all the time - including ourselves

- but, under no circumstance, or with any mask, could we fool God.

> *Lord, you search me and you know me... you discern my purpose from afar... all my ways lie open to you...*
> *(Ps 138:1-3)*

With the application of that thought, and with prayer, I could open up fully and frankly to him - there was absolutely no point in ducking any issues - and a lot of what I saw I did not particularly like, but at very least it made me aware of my shortcomings.

> *Being admonished to return to myself I entered in to my own depths, with you as guide, and I was able to do it because you were my helper.*
>
> (St Augustine)

A Journey of Surprises

That whole journey was also one of twists and turns, contrasts and surprises - spiritual, social and material. Some of the pilgrim accommodation was sublime either in location, or comfort and facilities; some was frankly awful. For the former I was very thankful, and for the latter, grateful that it was only for one night! They ranged from a lovely, hospitable convent, where we had separate rooms with basins and clean white sheets and big fluffy duvets, and a slap-up meal, to the most dilapidated, run-down, unsupervised school building on a noisy, dusty main road, with cranky beds and the most primitive of facilities; but they all served.

I am often asked if I ever got bored. I never did: when alone, there was lots to look at, think about, and take in. And at a walking pace, life does slow down to allow you to savour moments and sights at some length and in detail. There was also plenty of time for unhurried reflection, meditation or prayer. My mind could go into freewheel, in a leisurely and unstructured manner, because there was no obvious pressure for immediate resolution, and if a question was not resolved, I could quite happily "park" it and return to it another time.

> Pilgrimages lead to the tent of meeting with the Word of God. The fundamental experience of the pilgrim must be that of listening... The proclamation, reading and meditation of the Gospel must accompany the steps of the pilgrim and the visit to the shrine itself, so that what the Psalmist affirmed may be accomplished: "Your word is a lamp to my feet, a light on my path".
>
> (*Ps* 119:105) (*Pilgrimage in the Great Jubilee*)

The other thing I learned was frequently to turn, stand still, and look back. This was not about looking backwards, but seeing where I had come from, and seeing it with a completely different perspective - which of course is applicable during our life's pilgrimage. There was also a practical aspect. Unlike the pilgrim of the Middle Ages, who had to tramp his weary way home, these were the only times at which I would get a look at the return route!

Arrival

If you came this way,
Taking any route, starting from anywhere,
At any time or at any season,
It would always be the same: you would have to put off
Sense and notion. You are not here to verify,
Instruct yourself, or inform curiosity
Or carry report. You are here to kneel
Where prayer has been valid.

(TS Eliot, *Four Quartets*, Quartet No 4)

"It's not about the arrival - it's the journey that counts," is a phrase often heard about pilgrimage. But that arrival was truly special. Attending the pilgrim Mass in the splendid cathedral of St James in Santiago with other "arrived" pilgrims, experiencing a huge sense of community and achievement, both individual and collective; the drama of the great, smoking-trailing, pendulating *botafumeiro*; joyful meetings with friends from previous encounters along the way. There were also the quiet and private moments of giving heartfelt thanks for safe arrival, as well as high-tech moments (such as my family back home seeing me waving at them from one of the cathedral's external webcams!).

> Pilgrimages also lead to the tent of the meeting with the Church, "assembly of those who are called together by the Word of God to form the people of God. Being nourished by the body of Christ, they themselves form the body of Christ".
>
> (*Pilgrimage in the Great Jubilee*)

I had never presumed anywhere along my journey that I would get to Santiago; my hope at the end of each day was the next day's safe travel to the next *refugio*. Halfway through, I had to stop for a few days with knee problems. I just placed that in the hands of the Lord, fully accepting with gratitude that if this was as far as he wanted to take me on this occasion, well, that was fine. Thankfully, with prayer, rest and medication I was fit to set off again, without a hint of any further trouble in the ensuing weeks.

But to me, on this particular pilgrimage, it was mainly about the journey, because I benefitted so much during that slow, steady process - and indeed progress - of listening and learning, of suffering and rejoicing, of having that sense of getting somewhere. The destination and arrival was the gilding, the confirmation.

Reflections on return

I was greeted on return with, "Welcome back to the real world!" My instant, unthinking riposte was, "No, I've just left the real world." On reflection I realised how rich but simple my pilgrim world had been. Our needs were modest, we carried all our worldly possessions on our backs; we hoped for a shower and a bed every night, and one good meal a day sufficed. I had no interest whatsoever in goings-on in the outside world. So, although I was delighted to get back to my family and home comforts, I was actually very reluctant to re-embrace the rest of the world at large. I knew that I had left behind a far better world, but sadly one that could not be sustained in this exact fashion for any length of time. However, I believe that it can be replicated daily by anyone, anywhere, in small but frequent measure, through creating the atmosphere and aura of pilgrimage in seeking moments of peace and tranquillity.

> *The longest journey is the journey inwards.*
>
> (Dag Hammarskjöld)

This can be achieved at the very least by going "to your private room... and pray to your Father" (*Mt* 6:6) every day, wherever and however that may be, even just for a short period; but we should employ the same single-mindedness we unthinkingly give to setting aside the time to watch our favourite TV programme.

Occasionally the benefit of going "away to some lonely place all by yourselves and rest for a while" (*Mk* 6:31) should be sought, with a quiet walk in the park or the country, ten minutes in your garden, a Quiet Garden day, or even a retreat. Through this process of daily prayer and reflection you can now start making your own pilgrimage - whether it be physical, or in the mind, or both - so that you can take your journey out of time, and start discovering what is truly real.

The choice is between the Mystery and the absurd. To embrace the Mystery is to discover the real. It is to walk towards the light, to glimpse the morning star, to catch sight from time to time of what is truly real.

(Basil Hume)

Tying it all together

One of the strange contradictions of modern life is that between its illusory promise to give us all we could possibly need (at a cost, of course!), and the widespread desire to seek, sometimes with real longing, that something beyond the mortal condition which comforts and reassures (and costs nothing). Amongst other manifestations of this are the ever rising numbers on pilgrimage.

Pilgrimage of whatever duration or frequency is a practical and demonstrable way of seeking. It is a sure way of putting beliefs and commitment into the crucible. It digs up answers from deep within. Whilst it can be physically uncomfortable, it provides spiritual reassurance and consolation. You can walk and talk, in largely uninterrupted measure with God. Give him an inch, and he will show you the mile. Go the mile and he will remain with you on your life's journey.

For the common goal of our life-pilgrimage is to reach the Eternal Kingdom. Sadly, we seem to lose sight of this in the clutter and bustle of life. If only we could see ourselves as pilgrims on the difficult, hazardous and uncomfortable journey of life, and were prepared to help others, as I experienced on my physical pilgrimage, then the material world could be kept in perspective.

> "Over all, the glory of the Lord will be a tent to give shade by day from the heat, refuge and shelter from the storm and the rain."
>
> (*Is* 4:6) (*Pilgrimage in the Great Jubilee*)

Pilgrimage through the Ages

Pilgrimages symbolise the experience of the *homo viator* who sets out, as soon as he leaves the maternal womb, on his journey through the time and space of his existence. This is the fundamental experience of Israel, which is marching towards the promised land of salvation and of full freedom; the experience of Christ who rose to heaven from the land of Jerusalem, thus opening the way towards the Father; the experience of the Church which moves on through history towards the heavenly Jerusalem; the experience of the whole of humankind which tends towards hope and fulness.

(*Pilgrimage in the Great Jubilee*)

This is today's powerful, all-embracing view of pilgrimage given in *The Pilgrimage in the Great Jubilee*. It eloquently summarises that overarching yearning to recognise and make that spiritual journey - whether it be singly or collectively - whether it be immediate, or the lifetime pilgrimage.

Early Days

The urge to make a physical pilgrim-journey goes back to the deepest recesses of human memory. Primitive tribespeople who had wandered from the influence of their local deity were often driven to return to their roots for divine assistance or inspiration. In pre-Christian days, the practice of journeying to holy places is well documented. The Egyptians journeyed to Bastet's shrine at Bubastis, the Greeks sought inspiration from Apollo at Delphi, the Inca massed to worship the sun at Cusco. An anonymous and contemporary poem painted on a factory wall along the Way of St James on the approach to Najera, in Spain, sums up this primitive urge:

> *The force that drives me / the force that draws me*
> *I am unable to explain / Only He Above knows!*

It is ironic that the first Christian pilgrimage was, and still is, made to the seeming ordinariness of an empty tomb - that from which Jesus rose; and it is this empty tomb that still commands the most interest. Those first pilgrims were perhaps local folk: a mixture of the plain curious and those who came to marvel, and believe.

There is no firm evidence of any great pilgrim movement to Jerusalem from further afield during the first three centuries after the death of Jesus. Believers, certainly

The Way of St James.

in the first century AD, were more preoccupied with the Parousia, the anticipated Second Coming of Christ. The new Church also devoted its energies to looking outwards and establishing itself, as instructed by Christ to "Go, therefore, make disciples of all the nations." (*Mt* 28:19).

The destruction of Jerusalem in 70 AD, and the spread of the early Church by dispersion throughout the Roman Empire also effectively distracted the young Christian Church from this embryonic focal point. With events such as the martyrdom of Sts Peter and Paul in Rome, and many others, during the Neronian persecutions of 64-67 AD, all paths, physically and spiritually, began to lead to Rome.

However, Jerusalem did come back into focus early in the fourth century, when Constantine the Great, the first Christian emperor, built the Church of the Holy Sepulchre on the site of the empty tomb. The subsequent pilgrimage to Jerusalem by his mother, the Empress Helena, also served to give it further prominence. Since those early days, Jerusalem has been, and will no doubt remain, the most significant Christian pilgrim site for the compelling reason expressed by Origen: "to walk in the footsteps of the Master".

The Growth of Pilgrimage

Apart from the increasing passage to Rome and the Holy Land, other forms of pilgrimage in the first millennium appear unstructured and fragmented. Pilgrimage in the early Church was often motivated by a desire for exile and the renunciation of civilisation. Hence, in this context, the hermit was regarded as a pilgrim soul by St Jerome, and the establishment of the very early monasteries was perceived as an extension of this principle of the "pilgrimage of exile". The mobile pilgrims of the times were those who left their homes, as did the exilic Irish monks of the sixth and seventh centuries, to wander without particular destination, on the principle of "exile for God's sake, and go not only to Jerusalem, but everywhere, for God is everywhere".

Late in the first and into the second millennium, all this began to change. The Church had consolidated into an organised power, centred on Rome. The Christianised Empire had expanded throughout Europe and up to the Baltic states, as well as to the East. Churches were being built or rebuilt, and overland routes were being further developed and extended. Pilgrimage began to be ritualised and formalised by such acts as the granting of indulgences; sinners and criminals were sentenced by church or court to undergo penitential pilgrimages. The cult of martyrs played a key part in the development of the reasons for pilgrimage; the places where martyrs' blood was shed were from the earliest days both protected and hallowed, and people travelled to these places to ask for courage for their own Christian witness.

Saints and their relics also played an important part. All shrines, graves and resting places of the Saints (no matter how obscure) were customarily places of veneration: places where belief in the resurrection of the body and the life everlasting was professed. Hence there were (and still are) a huge number of pilgrim destinations of varying popularity and significance. Healings and miracles which take place in these places, such as Lourdes, also serve to deepen this sense of Christ's promise of eternal life.

All these strands in the development of pilgrimage reveal a Church strengthening its identity and universality and, in more earthly terms, its political and economic power. The Middle Ages thus became the great age of pilgrimage. Rome and Jerusalem vied with each other, and Santiago de Compostela came to rank with these two as one of the great destinations of medieval pilgrimage.

Dangers and Preparations

But whatever its goal, the pilgrim journey was typically a lengthy and hazardous affair. The pilgrim routes were badly constructed and poorly marked, crossing harsh, unforgiving and often mountainous terrain, with accompanying extremes of weather and, in remote areas, wild beasts. Safe passage was by no means assured, as in the frequent isolated areas, robbers and bandits preyed. In populated areas pilgrims were open to more insidious threats such as unscrupulous innkeepers, and pseudo-pilgrims or *coquillards* who befriended and then robbed their erstwhile companions.

Wars often disrupted or closed pilgrim routes. Disease was rife, treatment haphazard. Food and fodder were scarce. But to many, this was all grist to the mill: the more hazardous the route, the greater the merit and grace. Pilgrims were also expected to journey in a state of poverty; to quote the anonymous Russian author of the much later *Way of the Pilgrim*, "My possessions are a sack on my shoulders with a bit of dry bread and a Holy Bible that I carry under my shirt. No other thing do I have."

The prudent pilgrim, then, made thorough arrangements before setting off. He was required to make amends to all those he had offended or deprived. A sincere confession should then follow, otherwise the pilgrimage, for all its physical and moral accomplishments, would be spiritually worthless. A pilgrim's will had a special and protected status. A specific length of time might be determined, on the expiry of which he would be deemed deceased, and his wife free to remarry. The pilgrim, with his staff and scrip (leather pouch), would certainly expect a blessing before his final departure.

Hospitality

Amongst all these vicissitudes, the one glimmer of relief for the pilgrim was the hope of hospitality along the way, "for all pilgrims, rich or poor, who go to St James ought to be received with charity by all. Whoever receives them, receives St James and God himself", is the reassuring statement in the Pilgrim's Guide to Santiago, the *Codex Calixtinus*. The main burden in dispensing this hospitality naturally fell on the religious orders of the time. Hospitality is at the core of the Benedictine Rule. Other orders, if not dispensing charity, had specific tasks in support of the pilgrimage, such as the *Frères Pontifes*, who were responsible for building and maintaining bridges along the pilgrim route.

With the burgeoning demand from the hundreds of thousands of pilgrims along the major routes there were invariably, by the middle of the twelfth century, pilgrim hospices within a day's travel of each other. Life in these austere establishments was reported as "monstrous and uncomfortable". Some provided basic victuals; beds were a rarity, straw on the floor the norm. The well-off paid their way, others worked for their keep. The prize for hypocrisy must go to those wealthy folk who stayed smugly at home whilst their paid, proxy pilgrim endured the hazards and earned the indulgence for their benefactor.

There is also evidence that although pilgrims journeyed well beyond the confines of their highly localised lifestyle, pilgrimage itself was no great broadener of the mind. Pilgrims generally mistrusted and were unable to understand the local people; they in turn were regarded in the same light as today's modern tourist hordes: either as a nuisance, or as a means of making a lucrative living.

Controversy

By the late Middle Ages Rome was the most popular destination, chiefly through the presence of the Pope as St Peter's successor. There was, however, a pervading feeling that "tourism" thinly disguised as pilgrimage was beginning to be a motivating factor; by the fifteenth century, material curiosity was replacing deep spiritual motives. What was described as *curiositas*, worldly curiosity, prevented concentration on the divine.

Throughout the history of Christian pilgrimage, there also runs a thread of unease about the necessity of physical pilgrimage. St Augustine observed that, "not by journeying but by loving we draw nigh unto God. To him who is everywhere present and everywhere entire we approach not by our feet but by our hearts."

It was becoming obvious that however noble the pilgrimage concept was, and indeed nobly executed by many, the practicalities often fell far short of any Christian ideal. Corruption and fraud were at times endemic at all levels and all along the pilgrim routes. Unscrupulous innkeepers and fraudulent pardoners preyed on the gullible, and compounding this was widespread prostitution, an over-abundance of alcohol and other vices. It was not as though this was new, though, or had hitherto gone unnoticed; Gregory the Great in the sixth century recognised: "Rascality, adultery, theft, idolatry, poisoning, quarrelling and murder are rife".

Decline

The second half of the second millennium saw the decline of the great pilgrimages. There were many reasons for this. The Reformation played a principal part, particularly at the hands of those Reformers such as the arch-satirist Erasmus, who in his *Religious Pilgrimage* poured out contempt and derision on the abuses evident in the pilgrimage world.

Luther was more direct and persistent in his views: "Pilgrimages should be stopped" he said, and quoted *Acts* 4:12, "Only in him is there salvation; for 'of all the names in the world given to men, this is the only one by which we can be saved'". He advocated "justification by faith, not by pilgrimage". In keeping with the Reformers' overall views of man and his direct relationship with God through the Bible, perfect pilgrimage should therefore be a shift from external to internal, words replacing walking, meditation in place of marching.

The immediate effect of Reformation was an overall downturn in pilgrimages. There were few if any Protestant pilgrims, whilst Catholic pilgrimage continued in a subdued and diminished manner.

Renaissance

The fortunes of pilgrimage fluctuated during the seventeenth and eighteenth centuries. The Counter-Reformation added some stimulus, but the great era of massed pilgrimage had controversially and finally drawn to a close, dragged down by human voracity. But this muted end did not reckon with the mysterious human desire to make a physical journey to visit holy places.

The nineteenth and twentieth centuries saw a gradual renaissance in pilgrimage, from many directions and in many guises. Tourist travel was becoming safer and more widely available, and commercial tour operators saw a market for organised pilgrimages - Thomas Cook being one of the first. There was now a blurring of the distinction between pilgrim and tourist, mirroring that strange irony of those first visitors to the empty tomb - a combination of the curious and the devout.

There was also a resurgence of Protestant pilgrimage, inspired by scholastic and archaeological activities in Palestine after the First World War, which renewed interest in visiting the holy places. Evelyn Waugh described this ever-recurring desire: "The pilgrim's instinct is deep set in the human heart rather than of the head".

Another phenomenon brought new meaning, new destinations and new impetus to pilgrimage: the Apparitions of Our Lady, with her distinct call to prayer, at various places throughout the world. Lourdes in 1858 and Fatima in 1917 are two major examples. Much earlier, in 1531, she had appeared in Guadalupe, Mexico; the shrine there is reportedly the most visited Catholic pilgrim destination in the world, with over twelve million pilgrims going every year.

The Holy Land and Rome, for obvious reasons, remain at the fore, although the troubles in Palestine and Israel leave a continuing blight over the holy sites of the three big world faiths. Local pilgrimages flourish, such as those to Walsingham and Canterbury and their counterparts elsewhere in the world. Santiago de Compostela continues to increase in popularity; its particular appeal is that it is the one remaining pilgrimage with an established and frequent infrastructure along its main routes that not only caters for the modern pilgrim, but also reproduces the long distance walking pilgrimages of the Great Age.

"Life itself is a pilgrimage ..."

Pope Francis is very clear on the role of pilgrimage. In his Bull of Indiction declaring the Jubilee of Mercy (*Misericordiae Vultus*), he states:

> The practice of *pilgrimage* has a special place in the Holy Year, because it represents the journey each of us makes in this life. Life itself is a pilgrimage, and the human being is a *viator*, a pilgrim travelling along the road, making his way to the desired destination. Similarly, to reach the Holy Door in Rome or in any other place in the world, everyone, each according to his or her ability, will have to make a pilgrimage. This will be a sign that mercy is also a goal to reach and requires dedication and sacrifice. May pilgrimage be

an impetus to conversion: by crossing the threshold of the Holy Door, we will find the strength to embrace God's mercy and dedicate ourselves to being merciful with others as the Father has been with us.

Pilgrimage has found its place again. From those early Christians who were making their allegorical journey to re-enact the life of Christ, to the pilgrim of the Middle Ages caught up with the desire to seek pardon and indulgence, to the modern pilgrim-tourist who goes for a great variety of reasons, ranging from *curiositas* to deep devotion. There is every sign that this trend will continue, as that deep, innate desire still remains within us, with our continuing inability to explain the mysterious "force that draws us". But draw us it does.

Thus far did I come laden with my sin,
Nor could aught ease the grief that I was in
Till I came hither.
What a place is this!
Must here be the beginning of my bliss?
Must here the burden fall off from my back?
Must here the strings that bound it to me crack?
Blest Cross! Blest Sepulchre! Blest, rather, be
The Man that there was put to shame for me!
(John Bunyan, *The Pilgrim's Progress*)

Three Principal Pilgrim Places

The Holy Land and Jerusalem, Rome, and Santiago de Compostela were the most prominent pilgrim destinations of the Middle Ages. Jerusalem and the Holy Land, the crucible of Christianity, and Rome, its cradle, retain that prominence. Arguably, Santiago as well - for in this modern age it provides the last remaining long-distance pilgrim route that has adequate facilities to support the pilgrim, in the true spirit of pilgrimage, along the Way of St James.

THE HOLY LAND AND JERUSALEM

Be glad and rejoice for ever and ever for what I am creating, because I now create Jerusalem "Joy" and her people "Gladness".

(*Is* 65:18)

Of all Christian pilgrim destinations, the Holy Land must surely be the most desired. Countless millions of pilgrims have continuously journeyed there, during bad times and good, over the two millennia of Christian history, and still do so. Since the first day of the empty tomb, when a miraculous resurrection from an ignoble and miserable death was witnessed and reported, pilgrims have gone to that sacred spot to ponder, wonder and believe.

The Holy Sepulchre, Tomb of the Resurrection.

A pilgrimage to the Holy Land will allow you, in St John Paul II's words, to "go in search of the 'footprints' of God in that land rightly called holy, pursuing them, as it were in the stones, the hills, the waters which provided the setting for the earthly life of the Son of God...".

In that search you can follow Jesus's life: you can marvel at the Annunciation in the beautiful, modern Basilica in Nazareth, give thanks for his birth in the ancient Cave of the Nativity in Bethlehem, follow his ministry in the lovely churches and locations round the Sea of Galilee. You can ascend Mount Tabor to commemorate the Transfiguration, and experience the vibrant, exciting City of Old Jerusalem. Here there are many places to serve the pilgrim journey: from the Mount of Olives across the Kidron valley; the sombre Church of All Nations and the Garden of Gethsemane; Mount Zion with the Dormition Abbey, the Tomb of David, the Upper Room, and the Church of St Peter in Gallicantu, with, nearby, the original Maccabee Steps up which Jesus walked. And many other places besides....

The apogee, though, must be at the extraordinary church complex of the Holy Sepulchre: the scene of the Crucifixion and Resurrection, where you have the privilege and the grace of being in the very place where Jesus Christ, true God and true man, suffered, died and rose from the dead. You can also follow the Via Dolorosa, the authentic Stations of the Cross, through the crowded streets and alleyways of the Old City.

There is a danger of the Holy Land becoming isolated through misperceptions and faint hearts, leaving it to fall into disuse, and eventually diminish to fond memory and folklore. Let us earnestly consider Cardinal Cormac Murphy-O'Connor's "fervent plea for Christians to go on pilgrimage to the Holy Land, not only for their benefit, but also for the benefit of the Christian people of the Holy Land, many of whom have suffered much hardship because of the continuing conflict there." We owe it to this unique, irreplaceable, very Holy Land, from where our Christian faith came to light and life. We owe it to ourselves.

Go to immerse yourself in the spirit and ministry of Jesus as you relive the events; to give Christian witness and numbers in this tumultuous meeting place of the three great Abrahamic faiths; to support the Christian community, particularly in Bethlehem.

ROME

...and you, who believe in Christ, when you arrive in this City, you will able almost to touch with your own hands the wonderful miracle of you being a Christian, of your belonging to the Church.

(Cardinal Etchegaray)

Nowhere except Rome portrays the story of Christianity on such an expansive and vivid, yet compact tapestry. It presents a wealth of physical evidence reaching back through the millennia. This may bring to light in us fresh sentiments and perspectives about our Christian faith, as seen through the places, people and events that drove it forward and continue to do so, in such a powerful and enduring manner.

There are many advantages of a pilgrimage to Rome. It is accessible, and is straightforward to get about by foot, bus, or Metro; it is a compact city, so you can cover a lot of ground quickly. But there is such a lot to see and do that you could be overwhelmed, unless you plan your itinerary carefully (see the CTS booklet *Rome, A Pilgrim's Companion*).

St Peter's: take time to examine carefully this extraordinary church; to venerate the first Chief Shepherd, along with two of the most recent - St John XXIII and St John Paul II; to climb up the dome for amazing views of Rome; and take time out to pray in the quiet Adoration chapel. Special application has to be made to visit the Scavi - the underground excavations and site of St Peter's tomb - as daily numbers are restricted. Visit the beautiful Sistine chapel, but allow time for the many distractions when passing through the Vatican Museum to get to it!

Devotees of Our Lady are spoilt for choice, with many beautiful churches dedicated to her; foremost amongst them is the Basilica of St Mary Major. The Catacombs of Saint Callistus are a "must", where you will experience the deep and visibly expressed spirituality of those early and

View of St Peter's Square from the Basilica.

courageous Christians. Other compelling venues are St Paul's Outside the Walls, St John Lateran, and the Church of the Holy Cross in Jerusalem where relics from the Passion are on display. There are many other places: the iconic Colosseum, the Pantheon, the layers of Christian history in the church of St Clement…

Then there are the ongoing "live" events in St Peter's Square, where you will experience the huge buzz, and living universality of the Church, at the sizeable gatherings for the Holy Father's Wednesday audience, the Sunday Angelus, or the Sunday International Mass at St Peter's.

There are convents which offer reasonably priced, modest accommodation, and within easy reach of the Vatican.

Go to seek inspiration from the people and the places of the millennia of Christian history; to meet, celebrate and pray with the Universal Church, and the Chief Shepherd.

THE WAY OF SAINT JAMES AND SANTIAGO DE COMPOSTELA

There is no eternal city for us in this life but we look for one in the life to come.

(*Heb* 13:14)

After the declaration by the Bishop of Iria Flavia in the late ninth century that remains found in a Christian burial site were those of the first Apostle-Martyr, St James the

Santiago de Compostela.

Greater, pilgrims have been travelling the Way of St James
to what is now Santiago de Compostela for well over a
millennium. During all this time, Santiago was regarded
as the third most prominent pilgrimage destination after
Jerusalem and Rome.

Many of the historical routes still exist and are used,
but the major functioning, contemporary pilgrims' way
through France is the *Chemin de St Jacques* (GR 65)
which, when starting from Le-Puy-en-Velay in France's
Haute Loire, covers about nine hundred miles; or, if
you start at the border with Spain at St-Jean-Pied-de-
Port, covers about four hundred and fifty miles along
the *Camino Frances*, known simply as the "Camino",
to Santiago.

The GR 65 and Camino is the last of the long-distance
pilgrim routes that is geared for foot (and bicycle) pilgrims
with frequent and low-cost *gîtes d'étapes* (in France) and
refugios or *albergues* in Spain. Along this route you can
truly take time out of time. The walking route in France
passes through beautiful places and scenery; in Spain it
is more functional, but there are some lovely contrasting
places, with the wide open spaces and big skies of the
meseta, and the attractive, cosy greenery of Galicia.

The destination is the glorious Romanesque eleventh-
century cathedral, where St James's remains are
enshrined. Here you join the other "arriving" pilgrims
to celebrate your journey's end at St James's shrine, and

attend the daily pilgrim Mass, marvelling at the spectacle of the huge *botafumeiro* (thurible) being ceremonially swung right across the width and the height of this magnificent church.

As an 'arriving' pilgrim, though, you may reflect that it is not so much the arrival, but all those amazing, cumulative experiences and memories of the journey which make this so special.

Go to take time out of time; contemplate and discover as you journey; celebrate and give thanks on arrival; put into practice what you discovered on your return home.

Marian Shrines

Lourdes

> *O Most Holy Mother of my Jesus, you who saw and felt the extreme desolation of your dear Son, help me in my own time of desolation.*
>
> (St Bernadette)

Lourdes is one of the best-known pilgrim destinations in modern Christendom. For it was here in 1858 that Our Lady appeared to Bernadette, an impoverished, teenage girl, to impart her message of poverty, penance and prayer, and ultimately, hope and healing. Since then, pilgrims have been drawn by that message, seeking healing and hope.

Set in the northern foothills of the Pyrenees, Lourdes is a busy, international destination, but do not let the surrounding, commercial "busy-ness" (or reports thereof) put you off. For at the heart of Lourdes is the Domain, some fifty-two hectares of beautifully kept grounds and buildings, where there is always calm and dignity, and where there are plenty of quiet corners for prayer and reflection. The noticeable presence of the sick, infirm and disabled vividly establishes them as the Domain's "VIPs".

Grotto of Our Lady of Lourdes.

There are plenty of places for your devotions. There is the graceful basilica, which is in fact three separate churches: the Crypt, the Basilica of the Immaculate Conception, and the Rosary Basilica, all fronting the large concourse on which many events are staged. The spiritual heart of the Domain, though, is the Grotto of Massabielle, the cave by the River Gave, where Our Lady appeared to Bernadette. Amidst a blaze of candles, and gazing up at the iconic statue of Our Lady of Lourdes, pilgrims kneel or sit, rapt in prayer and reflection.

The rest of the Domain includes the huge, underground Basilica of St Pius X; the Chapel of Reconciliation and its attendant forty-eight multilingual confessionals; the Chapel of St Joseph; the large modern church of St Bernadette; and a small Adoration chapel. Lastly, there are the ice-cold Immersion Baths, fed from the spring unearthed by Bernadette at Our Lady's instruction, where many seek the healing waters. It is an extraordinary experience, and highly recommended. On the wooded hillside just outside the Domain are dramatic, life-sized Stations of the Cross.

Apart from the many Masses and other devotions, there are two major daily (seasonal) events - the Blessing of the Sick, and the candlelit Rosary procession, faithful testament to Our Lady's exhortation to Bernadette: "Tell the priests and people to come here in procession".

Other places of interest outside the Domain are the *cachot*, the former prison cell where the Soubirous family lived; their former home, Boly Mill; and, outside the town, Bartres, where Bernadette lived and tended sheep during her childhood.

Lourdes is a place of miracles, with countless untold healings of those who have experienced God's power; and those told, and verified by the Church, sixty-nine so far, where inexplicable and instantaneous healings of incurable conditions have occurred.

Go to seek healing and hope.

FATIMA

Fatima will always have something to say: the content of the message which the Virgin entrusted to the shepherd children and through them, to all men and women of our time. This is why the prophecy is not over, and never will be!

(Cardinal Martins of Portugal)

Fatima is a major, world-renowned Marian shrine in central Portugal. It commemorates six appearances of Our Lady to three local shepherd children at the Cova da Iria in 1917, and reiterates the messages given by her to them.

The main messages are of prayer, penance, reparation, daily recitation of the Rosary, and sacrifice. But also entwined are the more enigmatic "Three Secrets", which concern prophecy, eschatology, World War II, the consecration of Russia to the Immaculate Heart of Mary and the fall of Communism.

Fatima is a compact Sanctuary. At its spiritual heart is the simple, glass-sided Chapel of the Apparitions housing the iconic statue of Our Lady of Fatima, marking the exact spot of the Apparitions. It is unfussy, minimalist, resonant with the silence of the pilgrims sitting or kneeling in prayer. The most striking building in the Sanctuary is the majestic Basilica of Our Lady of the Rosary, where the three shepherd children are interred in this neo-classical church.

Standing in the centre of the huge concourse, twice the size of St Peter's Square, is a beautiful gold statue of the Sacred Heart of Jesus, symbolically placed over a spring found there. On the south side of the Sanctuary is a segment of the Berlin Wall as visible gratitude for God's intervention in the fall of communism.

To accommodate the large numbers of pilgrims coming to Fatima there is the massive, modern, circular Basilica of the Most Holy Trinity, at the opposite end of the Sanctuary. Adoration takes place in the Chapel of the Blessed Sacrament.

Fatima is a place of great significance in shaping modern history with regard to conflict and peacemaking. The messages of Our Lady of Fatima are ever more relevant as a focal point for the Church's mission of evangelisation in the third millennium.

Shrine of Our Lady of Fatima.

Go to reflect on, be immersed in, and learn from Our Lady's messages at source; and rediscover the Rosary!

GUADALUPE

When the image of the Virgin appeared on the tilma of Juan Diego, it was the prophecy of an embrace: Mary's embrace of all the peoples of the vast expanses of America...

(Pope Francis)

Christianity and the conversion of the local Aztec Indians came to Mexico with the Spanish conquest in 1519-21. In 1531, Our Lady appeared to an Indian convert, St Juan Diego, on Tepeyac Hill, now a suburb of Mexico City. As proof of her message to build a shrine there, she told Juan Diego to take some unseasonal roses to the local Bishop, which he wrapped in his cloak (tilma). On his opening the tilma to the Bishop, imprinted on it was a life-size image of Our Lady.

The cloak is made with the traditional cactus fibres with an average life-span of thirty years - but today the fabric is still as fresh and the image as clear as it was almost five hundred years ago. It is rich in Aztec symbolism, including a sign of pregnancy; hence Our Lady of Guadalupe's role as Patroness of the Unborn and as a commonly used icon of the Pro-Life movement.

Basilica of Our Lady of Guadalupe.

Guadalupe is claimed as the most visited Christian pilgrim site in the world. Dominating the Sanctuary is the huge, very striking, modern, circular Basilica, with a green copper roof thrown over it like an elegant cape. The tilma and image are displayed high above the main altar, where ingenious contra-directional, concealed walkways enable visitors to view it fully, without the obstruction of large standing crowds.

Next door is the ornate, original Antigua (Old) Basilica, dating from 1536. Owing to subsidence the whole building is tilted. It houses popular religious art, as well as many *ex voto* offerings for miracles and favours received. Also in the Sanctuary is the Chapel of the Fountain, a large auditorium, visitor information centre, and a museum.

Go to celebrate motherhood and the sanctity of life.

WALSINGHAM "ENGLAND'S NAZARETH"

Walsingham exists to remind us of the mystery of Mary's silent surrender, her self-sacrificing love, her joy and humility in bearing and believing the Word of God.

(*Community of Our Lady of Walsingham*)

In 1061 a Norfolk noblewoman, Richeldis de Faverches, was led in spirit by Our Lady to Nazareth, who showed and asked her to build a replica of the house where the

Statue of Our Lady of Walsingham.

Annunciation took place. A simple, wooden "Holy House" was built in Walsingham, and soon became the special focus of pilgrimage. In 1153 the Augustinians founded a Priory in the vicinity of the Holy House, as Walsingham became one of the prominent pilgrim destinations of medieval Christendom. During the Dissolution in 1538, the Priory was closed and the Holy House destroyed. Nothing remains today of the original shrine, but the site is marked out on the lawn in the "Abbey Grounds" in Walsingham, where we also find the Priory ruins.

In 1896, Miss Charlotte Boyd, an heiress, bought and restored the Slipper Chapel at the nearby hamlet of Houghton St Giles. This chapel was built in 1340 and survived the Dissolution intact; it was the last "station" where pilgrims stopped to remove their shoes before walking barefoot along the "Holy Mile" to the shrine in Walsingham.

The first public pilgrimage came to the Chapel in 1897, and with passing years pilgrim numbers grew. The first Mass there since the Reformation was celebrated in 1934, and, at a large pilgrimage in 1938, the Slipper Chapel was declared the Roman Catholic National Shrine of Our Lady.

The site is in the tranquil countryside of Norfolk. Enthroned in the diminutive Slipper Chapel is the iconic statue of Our Lady of Walsingham. Adjoining the Slipper Chapel is the Holy Spirit Chapel, which is usually a blaze of pilgrims' prayer candles. Nearby is the handsome, modern Chapel of Reconciliation, built in the style of a typical Norfolk barn, where pilgrim services are held. There is a shop, café and picnic area in the grounds.

In the picturesque village of Walsingham is the striking, newly-built Parish Church of the Annunciation. Here also, is the Anglican Shrine to Our Lady, with a replica of the Holy House.

Go to "England's Nazareth", and share Mary's great joy and inner peace of the Annunciation.

PARIS - RUE DE BAC

Have a medal made according to this model. Everyone who wears it around their neck will receive great graces.

(Our Lady to St Catherine Labouré)

In the 7th Arondissement of Paris, at number 140, Rue de Bac is the Chapel of Our Lady of the Miraculous Medal. Here, a twenty-four year old novice sister, Catherine Labouré, experienced three apparitions of Our Lady in 1830, and was given the mission of establishing devotion to the Miraculous Medal, a devotion that is now worldwide.

The beautiful, ornate, light chapel depicts the apparitions in great detail. Although the medal was struck and propagated by the Archbishop of the time, who immediately understood its import, Catherine's identity as the recipient of the apparitions was not known until after her death over forty years later. Her incorrupt body lies peacefully in the Chapel.

Go to acquire your Miraculous medal "at source"; and then seek those graces promised by Our Lady in the prayerful atmosphere of this sublime place.

BANNEUX

I come to relieve suffering. (Our Lady of Banneux)

Eleven year-old Mariette Beco from the hamlet of Banneux, Belgium experienced eight apparitions of Our Lady in 1933. Our Lady described herself as "The Virgin of the Poor". In one of the apparitions she told Mariette to plunge her hands into a small spring, which was for healing and "for all nations", giving rise to the title, "Our Lady of All Nations", although her primary title is "Our Lady of the Poor".

This is a lovely, peaceful site, set in the Ardennes woodland. The Chapel of the Apparitions is the focal point, with the nearby spring still flowing freely. There are many small chapels, statues (including Our Lady of Walsingham), Stations of the Cross and other devotional objects dotted around for prayer and contemplation, many reflecting the "all nations" aspect. The church of the Virgin of the Poor serves larger gatherings. Masses, Adoration, Rosary, Confessions and Anointing of the Sick are available, subject to season.

Go to meet Our Lady of the Poor, and pray with her for all nations.

LA SALETTE

La Salette is a message of hope, for our hope is nourished by the intercession of her who is the Mother of mankind.

(St John Paul II)

High in the alpine pasture of the French Alps lies the Shrine of Our Lady of La Salette - in a glorious, remote, tranquil location. Our Lady appeared here in 1846 to two young shepherd children, with a message of turning away from sin, and seeking repentance and conversion.

This is a completely "self-contained" site, with an imposing, late-nineteenth-century basilica and associated devotional activities and pilgrim accommodation. Hiking trails abound in this beautiful, peaceful place.

Go to immerse yourself in Our Lady's peaceful presence, surrounded by God's most natural and grand-scale handiwork.

LORETO

The happy House of Nazareth is justly regarded and honoured as one of the most sacred monuments of the Christian Faith.

(Pope Leo XIII)

Ancient tradition recounts that the Holy House of Loreto, near Ancona in Italy, is the same dwelling place in Nazareth in which Our Lady received the Annunciation. It was transported by angelic interventions at various times to various places to save it from destruction, and ended up at Loreto in 1294. It has since been a popular place of pilgrimage, visited by many Popes and Saints.

This intriguing, diminutive, three-sided, rough-bricked building displays traces of mediaeval murals and Judeo-Christian graffiti. The house is enclosed by an ornate Bramantian Renaissance marble screen, which in turn sits in the imposing, domed fifteenth century Basilica.

Go in the spirit of faith to enter into Mary's house, and pray for the graces of the Annunciation.

KNOCK

I have felt a strong desire to come here, the desire to make yet another pilgrimage to the Shrine of the Mother of Christ, the Queen of Peace.

(Pope St John Paul II on his visit to Knock, 1979)

In County Mayo, Ireland, in August 1879 in the small village of Knock, a three hour silent and static apparition of Our Lady, flanked by St Joseph and St John the Evangelist, with, behind them, a lamb on an altar, was seen by villagers on the gable end of the parish church of St John the Baptist.

Today, pilgrims come to Knock from all over the world. The original parish church incorporates a separate, tasteful Adoration chapel, and nearby is the modern, sizeable basilica which serves larger pilgrim groups. There are also Blessed Sacrament and Reconciliation chapels, and Stations of the Cross.

Go to seek "the Way, the Truth and the Life".

EPHESUS - THE HOUSE OF THE VIRGIN MARY

From here in Ephesus, a city blessed by the presence of Mary Most Holy - who we know is loved and venerated also by Muslims - let us lift up to the Lord a special prayer for peace between peoples.

(Pope Benedict XVI)

Tradition has it that Our Lady was taken by St John the Evangelist, to whom Our Lord entrusted her at the Crucifixion ("This is your mother" *Jn* 19:27), to this small house on Mount Koressos, not far from the ancient city of Ephesus, now in the province of Izmir in western Turkey, and here she spent the rest of her days.

The house was discovered in the nineteenth century following descriptions given by the German nun and visionary Blessed Anne Catherine Emmerich. The shrine has merited several Apostolic Blessings and visits from Popes, most recently Pope Benedict XVI. A steady flow of pilgrims - Muslim, Western and Eastern Christians - make their way to this small, charming, ancient stone chapel to pray, physically to leave their prayers with the thousands of others on the "Wall of Wishes", and drink water from the spring.

Go to contemplate "your Mother"; and to "Lift up to the Lord a special prayer for peace among peoples".

The Great Saints

St Pio of Pietrelcina - San Giovanni Rotondo

One of the towering - and controversial - figures of this age was St Pio of Pietrelcina ("Padre Pio") (1887-1968), Franciscan Friar, stigmatic and mystic.

He is celebrated in the southern Italian town of San Giovanni Rotondo, where he ministered for many years. Within a sizeable pilgrim complex is the original (1959) church of Santa Maria delle Grazie, and behind that, to cater for ever growing numbers of pilgrims, is the huge, most arresting modern architecture of the Padre Pio Pilgrimage church (2004). Within and around these churches you can view his cell, his confessional, the crucifix from which he received his stigmata, and his incorrupt body. On the hillside above Santa Maria are beautifully executed Stations of the Cross.

Go to "Pray, pray to the Lord with me, because the whole world needs prayer." (St Pio)

St Thérèse of Lisieux - Lisieux

Lisieux is a charming Normandy town whose most famous daughter, St Thérèse of the Child Jesus and the Holy Face (1873-1897), died in the obscurity of the Carmelite convent there, not knowing that her wish to be a world missionary would be uniquely fulfilled through her widely published autobiography, *The Story of a Soul*.

Lisieux is redolent of St Thérèse, with a massive, neo-Byzantine basilica dedicated to her, a basilica which also houses the mortal remains of her parents, Blessed Louis and Zelie Martin, who will be canonized in October 2015. There is also the dignified, Gothic cathedral of St Peter, where the Martin family worshipped; Les Buissonets, the family home; and the Carmel, with its simple chapel. By the chapel in the Carmel is St Thérèse's reliquary, portraying her peaceful, serene figure on her death bed.

Go to seek the "Little Way" of St Thérèse.

ST FRANCIS OF ASSISI - ASSISI

St Francis of Assisi (1182-1226) was the soldier-son of a wealthy family, who gave up a hedonistic lifestyle, turned to the poor and sick, and rose to the challenge God put before him to "rebuild my church".

The Umbrian town of Assisi is a bustling, compact town through and around which the many strands of St Francis can be readily followed. There is the magnificent Basilica of St Francis, with a crypt housing his tomb; and the Basilica of St Clare, a noblewoman who renounced her life in the world to follow Francis into the way of poverty.

Just outside Assisi is the first Poor Clares' convent, and the diminutive chapel of St Damiano which St Francis literally rebuilt. On the slopes of Mount Subasio is the Carceri Hermitage, a small Franciscan monastery to which St Francis used to retreat and pray. On the plain below, is the sizeable Basilica of St Mary of the Angels, which encloses the original, tiny chapel of the Portiuncula, the second church that Francis rebuilt, and where he fully understood his vocation.

Go to seek inspiration to "rebuild your church".

ST JEAN-MARIE VIANNEY - ARS-SUR-FORMAN

Ars-sur-Forman was the village parish of its extraordinary priest, St Jean-Marie (John-Mary) Vianney, known simply as the Curé of Ars (1786-1859). He ministered by sheer dint of personal example and pastoral devotion, and was known as a "martyr to his confessional", drawing many people from far outside the parish.

This small village is well-geared to the pilgrim, with a neat, green-copper-domed basilica joined seamlessly to the original twelfth century parish church. The underground church of Our Lady of Mercy caters for more sizeable gatherings, and there is the Chapel of the Heart, and an Adoration chapel built by St Jean-Marie. Close by is his presbytery, with interesting personal artefacts.

St Jean-Marie is the patron saint of parish priests. Just outside the village is the seminary and Foyer Sacerdotal John Paul II for priests on retreat, of which the modern chapel is open to the public, and well worth a visit.

Go to seek reconciliation with God; or, to discern your vocation (to whatever calling).

St Mary Magdalene - La Sainte Baume
(The Holy Cave)

The Holy Cave, just east of Marseilles, is a large cavern high up on the cliff face of the Sainte Baume Massif, beautifully adapted as a church. Tradition has it that Mary Magdalene spent her last days here as a hermit.

It is a quiet, rugged area, off the tourist trail. Access is by a fifty minute or so walk along ever-ascending forest trails from the nearest car parks, through silent, cathedral-like forests. The church is a sublime place in which to worship and meditate.

Go to seek the tranquillity of this most unusual and beautiful place; to ponder on Mary Magdalene's life and ministry.

St Teresa of Jesus - Avila

St Teresa of Jesus (1515-1582), Carmelite nun, mystic, reformer of the Carmelite Order, female patron saint of Spain, theologian, and first female Doctor of the Church:

this formidable Spanish Saint is celebrated primarily at the Convent of St Teresa in Avila. Although an active convent, pilgrims can visit the site of her birthplace, now an elaborate chapel within the Baroque church. The *Sala de Reliquas* contains her relics and those of her collaborator, St John of the Cross. Her incorrupt heart and an arm are enshrined at the Carmelite convent of the Annunciation, in the nearby town of Alba de Tormes, where she died.

The second establishment at Avila is the Monasterio de la Encarnación, the Carmelite convent Teresa first entered. Here, pilgrims can view her monastic cell and other rooms associated with her, and in the courtyard is a visual representation of her writing *The Interior Castle*.

She left the Monastery of the Incarnation in 1562 to found her first reformed monastery, also at Avila: the Convent of St Joseph, birthplace of the Discalced Carmelites, which contains a museum dedicated to her.

May you trust God that you are exactly where you are meant to be.

(St Teresa of Avila)

Go in trust and thanksgiving that you are exactly where you are meant to be; or, if you need inspiration and courage radically to change your life.

ST ANTHONY OF PADUA - PADUA

Franciscan friar (1195-1231), distinguished preacher, kindred spirit of St Francis, Doctor of the Church, and patron saint of lost articles, St Anthony is commemorated at the imposing, multi-domed and turreted twelfth-thirteenth century Basilica of St Anthony in Padua; his remains are interred in the side chapel of his name.

There is plenty here for the pilgrim in this imposing cathedral with its welcoming Pilgrim Reception Office, many side chapels, and four attractive cloisters, its museums, exhibitions and shop. It is also the home of the popular publication *St Anthony's Messenger*.

> *Christians must lean on the Cross of Christ just as travellers lean on a staff when they begin a long journey.*
>
> (St Anthony of Padua)

Go as that traveller to lean on the Cross of Christ.

Other Pilgrim Places

This chapter briefly mentions a miscellany of other places, some well-known, others less so, and some challenging. They are in no particular order.

The CTS booklet *Pilgrim France* gives additional pilgrimage destinations in France.

THE SACRED HEART OF JESUS - PARAY-LE-MONIAL

In the seventeenth century the Lord chose your town to bring forth a new source of merciful and infinitely generous love on which generations of pilgrims will draw.

(St John Paul II)

In the picturesque rural town of Paray-le-Monial is a Visitandine convent, where, in 1673, Sister Margaret Mary Alacoque experienced the encounters with Christ that determined her mission of spreading devotion to his Sacred Heart throughout the world.

Pilgrims can attend services, or just pray and meditate in the peaceful convent chapel where Margaret Mary had her apparitions. Other pilgrim places are the handsome, twin-towered eleventh century Benedictine basilica, the outdoors "Green Cathedral", a lovely, barn-like Adoration chapel, and the unusual Jesuit church which commemorates St Claude de la Colombière and his association with St Margaret Mary's mission.

Go to seek and adore the Sacred Heart of Jesus at this source of revelation.

Taizé

Since my youth, I think that I have never lost the intuition that community life could be a sign that God is love, and love alone… a community where kindness of heart and simplicity would be at the centre of everything.

(Br Roger Schutz)

Founded by Brother Roger Schutz, Taizé, in the depths of Burgundy, has been described as "Christianity's best-kept secret". Taizé is a living, dynamic, religious community, dedicated to focusing on the essence of the Gospel. It principally invites attendance by, and speaks powerfully to, young people (between fifteen and twenty-nine), of whom millions have passed through in its seventy-five year history. Adults over thirty are also welcome, but with limits on time and numbers.

Life on the week-long programme is very simple: tented or dormitory-style accommodation, simple meals, daily chores, but underpinning it a daily rhythm of prayer and worship, reflection, and workshops, all permeated by the beautiful, melodic music synonymous with Taizé. The main worship sessions are held in the spacious Church of Reconciliation, largely seatless, ablaze with candles and adorned with icons. A welcoming and refreshing ecumenism and practice features large here, the various traditions celebrating a unified fellowship.

Go in a spirit of freedom, reconciliation and trust, and there you will experience acceptance.

OUR LADY OF GRACES AND ST JOSEPH - COTIGNAC

The small, attractive Provencal town of Cotignac has the unique distinction of having had not only a rare apparition of St Joseph, but also previously an (unconnected) apparition of Our Lady.

A small, simple, dignified basilica commemorates the appearance of "Our Lady of Graces" in 1519. It has extensive terraced grounds with plenty of nooks and crannies to seek peace and quiet. Traditionally, through events that link Our Lady of Graces with the birth of Louis XIV to Queen Anne, childless couples bring their intercessions here.

Within walking distance of Our Lady of Graces is the chapel and grotto that remembers St Joseph's appearance in 1660. The chapel is served by the Benedictine sisters of the adjoining convent, and pilgrims are welcome to attend their daily services. The exterior grotto is accessible at all hours, and from it the waters that were uncovered at St Joseph's behest still flow.

For those seeking the gift of children; for devotees of Mary and Joseph.

Canterbury Cathedral

And specially from every shires ende
Of Engelond to Caunterbury they wende,
The hooly blisful martir for to seke,
That hem hath holpen whan that they were seeke.
(Geoffrey Chaucer, Canterbury Tales)

A church has stood in Canterbury since 597, founded by the missionary St Augustine, sent from Rome. Like all the ancient churches in England it experienced a turbulent history, living through many cycles of destruction and reconstruction; what has emerged is today's immense, glorious eleventh-twelfth century Romanesque-Gothic cathedral, with its stunning stained glass windows.

It has long been a pilgrim destination, particularly after the murder of Thomas Becket on Henry II's orders in

1170; it was famously celebrated by Chaucer's *Canterbury Tales* (late fourteenth century). Although the well-worn medieval Pilgrim's Way from Winchester has largely been obscured by today's roads, there is a modern Pilgrim's Way that can be followed.

Go to pray for Christian unity, to strengthen a true desire to be "All one in Christ Jesus." (*Ga* 3:28)

POLAND - AUSCHWITZ AND THE DIVINE MERCY

Here are two unusual, starkly contrasting but linked pilgrim destinations: one, at Auschwitz (Oświęcim), depicting the grim brutality of man's inhumanity, and the other God's limitless and unconditional mercy, as portrayed at the Shrine of the Divine Mercy at Łagiewniki, Kraków.

Auschwitz is a forbidding, terrible place, but as a presentation of this awful inhumanity of man it is sensitively and thoughtfully organised. Similarly the huge, adjoining basic accommodation site of Birkenau, where crematoria also operated, is grim but salutary viewing.

One can find blessed relief at the Shrine of the Divine Mercy just outside Kraków. This is the convent of St Faustina, the Polish nun who received the instruction and messages of the Divine Mercy from Our Lord. The site is now based round the magnificent, stately Basilica of the Divine Mercy and associated facilities.

A short walk away is the newly built John Paul II Centre, designated as the principal shrine to St John Paul II, but also providing a wide range of facilities.

Go to Auschwitz to confront man's inhumanity; and to the Shrine of Divine Mercy to be reassured of God's unconditional mercy.

THE SHROUD OF TURIN

A truly mysterious image, which no human artistry was capable of producing. In some inexplicable way, it appeared imprinted upon cloth and was believed to show the true face of Christ, the crucified and risen Lord.

(Cardinal Ratzinger, later Pope Benedict XVI)

The provenance of the Shroud before the sixteenth century is untraceable. The first definitive record of it is in 1578, when it was brought to Turin from France. Since then countless pilgrims have been drawn to this garment with its powerful, evocative image, to gaze with faith on the Crucified Christ.

The Shroud is housed in the Chapel of the Shroud in Turin Cathedral. It is only put on public display in the cathedral for pre-announced limited periods. Ten minutes walk from the Cathedral is the associated Holy Shroud Museum, with a wealth of detail and illustrations of the Shroud and its history.

Go and "allow ourselves to be reached by this look, which is directed not to our eyes but to our heart." (Pope Francis)

MARTHE ROBIN - CHATEAUNEUF-DE-GALAURE:

Deep in the Department of Drôme is the typical "crossroads" French village of Chateauneuf-de-Galaure, which is not yet formally recognised as an "official" place of pilgrimage. Pilgrims, however, come privately to pay their respects to Venerable Marthe Robin (1902-1981), stigmatic and mystic, who was born, lived and died here in acute life-long suffering and obscurity. Her legacy is manifestly obvious in this village, and around the world, in her foundation of the Foyers of Charity.

At Chateauneuf you can visit the founding Foyer. Whilst it is not specifically geared to handling influxes of pilgrims, they will only be too happy to talk about Marthe and her life and ministry, as well as to direct you to Ferme Robin, where Marthe spent her entire life. In this small, neat farmhouse you can sit for a while in Marthe's quite ordinary bedroom, and contemplate and pray with her in spirit, reflecting on her extraordinary life.

Go to *"plunge into the love of the Lord"*
(Marthe Robin).

THE INFANT OF PRAGUE

The Infant Jesus of Prague is a small, sixteenth century, wax-coated and wooden statue held in the Carmelite Church of Our Lady Victorious in Prague, robed in rich vestments. The most recent crown adorning the statue is that gifted, and placed on the statue, by Pope Benedict XVI in 2009.

It is of Spanish origin, and tradition claims it once belonged to St Teresa of Avila. Once a precious family heirloom, it was presented to the Carmelite Church in Prague in 1628. It survived removals and destructions during the Thirty Years War. Since 1741 it has been continuously in Our Lady Victorious, and has drawn many devotees worldwide. Many favours, blessings and miracles have been reported.

The part-Baroque, part-Renaissance church was built by the Lutherans in 1611. It was consecrated to Our Lady Victorious in 1624.

Go to kneel before this Infant, and realise how much a small child may move us with his need only for love.

THE HOLY ISLAND OF LINDISFARNE

Dry-shod, o' er sands, twice every day,
The pilgrims to the shrine find way:
Twice every day the waves efface
Of staves and sandaled feet the trace.

(Sir Walter Scott)

This tiny, tide-dependent island one mile off the north-east coast of England is an important centre of Celtic Christianity. First came the foundation of a monastery in 635 by St Aidan, an Irish monk from Iona. Later, with St Cuthbert, it became a base for the evangelisation of north-east England.

Apart from its picturesque and rugged setting, there is an abundance of riches for the pilgrim: the evocative ruins of the twelfth century Lindisfarne Priory; and a sixteenth century castle that dominates the island. There are a number of churches: the Anglican Parish Church of St Mary, on the site of the original monastery; St Aidan's Catholic Church, and St Cuthbert's United Reform. There are also retreat houses and centres for individuals and groups.

Go to exult in God's nature, and give thanks for the spread of Christianity.

MEDJUGORJE

A contemporary, popular destination in Bosnia Herzegovina, where it is claimed that apparitions, allegedly of the Virgin Mary, occur regularly to some local seers; they reportedly started in 1981.

These claims have not been approved by the Church, and Medjugorje is not endorsed as a destination for organised pilgrimage. However, millions have visited, and there have been many accounts of sincere conversion, acts of repentance and evident devotion.

If you go, go as private pilgrims, and in obedience to the Church's guidance, teaching and practice.

Pilgrim Prayer

I offer you this Pilgrim Prayer, to sum up the pilgrim experience, and which we may offer to God as we set off once more as that *viator* on our daily, and our life's, journey:

A Pilgrim's Prayer

Dear Lord - as I start my journey today:
open my eyes to your face in others;
keep them open to your glorious creation.
Open my ears to your Word;
keep them open so that I may hear what you say.
Open my mind to every encounter;
keep it open to what you are teaching me.
Open my heart to your love;
keep it open to love others.
Give me the courage to see myself as you see me,
and to tell you the story of my life that I
have never been able to tell anyone before.

As I follow the footsteps and sign-posts
of my pilgrimage,
illuminate more clearly the path away from sin,
to union with you.

Allow me a glimpse of Paradise through order,
peace, contemplation and love.
Bestow on me the wisdom to relegate self,
and the generosity to promote others;
my desire is "thy will", and not "my will".
My daily burden and pain I endure for you;
my joy I willingly give to you.
Grant that I reach my destination this day;
grant safe arrival every day.

Grant full revelation of the Mystery as I reach my
destination at the end of my life's pilgrimage.

In your great kindness grant all this to my fellow
pilgrims.
In your great mercy hear my prayer.

(David Baldwin)

Further Reading

In a book of this size, it would be impossible sensibly to list the vast quantity of (constantly shifting) information available on the internet about pilgrimage or pilgrim places. We can only recommend you start by searching for and engaging with the relevant official Shrine websites.

The Vatican document *Pilgrimage in the Great Jubilee* published in 1998, and approved by St John Paul II, is well worth reading for an in depth expose on the spiritual aspects of pilgrimage:

http://www.vatican.va/roman_curia/pontifical_councils/migrants/ documents/rc_pc_migrants_doc_19980425_pilgrimage_en.htm

The website of the British charity, The Confraternity of St James, is also well worth a visit, not only for those wishing to embark on the Way of St James, but for a good understanding of practical pilgrimage in general: *www.csj.org.uk*

For those contemplating pilgrimage to the Holy Land and Jerusalem the Christian Information Centre in Jerusalem offers much worthwhile information on its website: *www.cicts.org*

Most of these pilgrim places have very acceptable, associated pilgrim accommodation.

CTS publications relating to the pilgrim places mentioned:

D646   *The Message of Walsingham*, R W Connolly SM.

D652   *The Message of Guadalupe*, Gillian Rae

D653   *Santiago de Compostela*,
        The Pilgrim Way of St James, David Baldwin

D658   *The Message of Assisi*, Chris Simpson

D661   *Lourdes: a place of healing and hope*, David Baldwin

D676   *Rome: A Pilgrim's Companion*, David Baldwin

D684   *The Holy Land: A Pilgrim's Companion*, David Baldwin

D698   *Lourdes: Love is the cure*, Pope Benedict XVI

D706   *Lisieux: A Pilgrim's Companion*, David Baldwin

D718   *The Sacred Heart: A Pilgrim's Companion*, David Baldwin

D743   *Pilgrim France,* David Baldwin

D763   *Glastonbury: A Pilgrim's Companion*, David Baldwin

B746   *Brother Roger and Taizé*, Fr Bryan Wells.

SP23   *Message of Bernadette*, V Johnson & D Foley

D651   *What Happened at Fatima*, Leo Madigan

D696   *Poland*, David Baldwin

D751   *Litany of Loreto*, Rt Rev Charles Renfrew

D657   *Medjugorje*, David Baldwin

B679   *Anthony of Padua*, Fr Jude Winkler OFM Conv

B713   *Francis of Assisi*, Silvia Vecchini

B727   *Curé d'Ars*, George W Rutler

B686   *Clare of Assisi*, John Paul Kirkham

B652   *Marthe Robin*, PH Tierney M Blake & D Fanning

B706   *Teresa of Avila*, Jennifer Moorcroft

B204   *Thérèse of Lisieux*, Mgr Vernon Johnson

D707   *Little Way of St Thérèse*

D331   *Message of St Thérèse of Lisieux*, Mgr Vernon Johnson

D693   *Thérèse Teacher of Prayer*, Br Craig Driscoll

B709   *Louis & Zélie Martin*, Fr Paulinus Redmond

Do662   *Apparitions of Mary*, Donal Foley

D650   *Divine Mercy and St Faustina*, Fr Andrew Witko

D781   *Infant of Prague*, Glynn MacNiven Johnston

B702   *John of the Cross*, Jennifer Moorcroft